Divided By

by Marilyn Deen

Consultant:
Adria F. Klein, PhD
California State University, San Bernardino

CAPSTONE PRESS
a capstone imprint

Wonder Readers are published by Capstone Press,
1710 Roe Crest Drive, North Mankato, Minnesota 56003.
www.capstonepub.com

Library of Congress Cataloging-in-Publication Data
Deen, Marilyn.
    Divided by / Marilyn Deen.—1st ed.
        p. cm.—(Wonder readers)
    Includes index.
    ISBN 978-1-4296-9606-7 (library binding)
    ISBN 978-1-4296-7914-5 (paperback)
    1. Division—Juvenile literature. I. Title.
    QA115.D44 2013
    513.2'14—dc23   2011022018

Summary: Simple text and color photographs present the concept of division.

Note to Parents and Teachers

The Wonder Readers: Mathematics series supports national mathematics standards. These titles use text structures that support early readers, specifically with a close photo/text match and glossary. Each book is perfectly leveled to support the reader at the right reading level, and the topics are of high interest. Early readers will gain success when they are presented with a book that is of interest to them and is written at the appropriate level.

Printed in the United States of America in North Mankato, Minnesota.
042012   006682CGF12

Table of Contents

Big into Small

If you have 4 cars and you want to split them into 2 **equal groups**, you can do that. There will be 2 cars in each group. When you split a big group into smaller groups, you are dividing the big group.

In math, adding smaller groups together to make a big group is called addition.

Dividing big groups into smaller groups is called **division**.

Here is the number sentence that tells about the cars: $4 \div 2 = 2$. In words, we say, "Four divided by two equals two."

Solve the Problem

Here are 6 piggy banks. You can divide them into 2 equal groups. See if you can figure out how many banks would be in each group.

To write the number sentence that goes with this **problem**, you write: 6 ÷ 2 = 3.

To say this sentence in words, you say, "Six divided by two equals three."

The 6 banks can be divided into 2 groups of 3 each.

You have 8 red apples.
To divide them into 2 groups,
you divide 8 by 2.
You write this number sentence:
8 ÷ 2 = ?

You can split 8 apples into 2 groups if you put 4 in each group. In other words, 8 divided by 2 equals 4.

$8 \div 2 = 4$

You have 10 teddy bears
and you want to divide them
into 2 equal groups.
If you want to end up with
2 groups, then you divide by 2.
$10 \div 2 = ?$

There will be 5 teddy bears in each group when you divide 10 by 2. Or, put another way, 10 divided by 2 equals 5.

10 ÷ 2 = 5

If you divide 12 by 2, you will end up with 2 smaller groups. Dividing these 12 eggs by 2 means there will be 6 eggs in each group.

$12 \div 2 = 6$

There are other ways to divide 12 into groups. You might want 3 groups of eggs instead. You want to divide 12 by 3. When you divide 12 eggs into 3 groups, there will be 4 eggs in each group. 12 divided by 3 equals 4.

$12 \div 3 = 4$

Now You Try

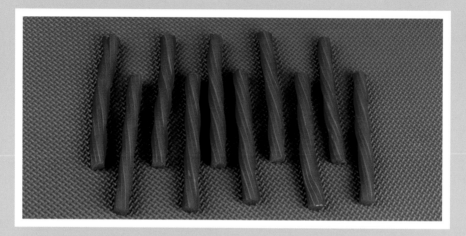

Count the number of candies.
Count the number of groups
of candies you see.
Say the number sentence
that tells how these candies
have been divided into groups.

There are 10 candies in 2 groups.
There are 5 candies in each group.
10 divided by 2 equals 5.
Or, if you write it with **numerals**,
this is how it looks:
10 ÷ 2 = 5

Here are 8 friends. If they want
to separate into 2 groups,
4 friends will be in each group.
Eight divided by 2 equals 4.
And now that you know all about
division, it's time for them to split!
Goodbye!

Now Try This!

Use a counter to demonstrate the division problems from the book. The teacher will write each number sentence from the book on the board or chart paper. Arrange your counter on your desks to illustrate each division problem. When you have worked through all of the sentences from the book, try working through a few additional simple division sentences that were not included in the book.

Glossary

divide to split something into two or more parts

division the act of dividing one number by another

equal the same as something else in size, value, or amount

group a number of things that go together or are similar in some way

numeral a written symbol that represents a number

problem a puzzle or question that needs to be solved

Internet Sites

FactHound offers a safe, fun way to find Internet sites related to this book. All of the sites on FactHound have been researched by our staff.

Here's all you do:

Visit *www.facthound.com*

Type in this code: 9781429696067

And go to Capstonekids.com for more about Capstone's characters and authors. While you're there, you can try out a game, a recipe, or even a magic trick.

Super-cool stuff!

Check out projects, games and lots more at
www.capstonekids.com

Index

Editorial Credits

Maryellen Gregoire, project director; Mary Lindeen, consulting editor; Gene Bentdahl, designer; Sarah Schuette, editor; Wanda Winch, media researcher; Eric Manske, production specialist

Photo Credits

Capstone Studio: Karon Dubke, all

Word Count: **469**   Guided Reading Level: **M**   Early Intervention Level: **18**